Original title:
A Symphony of Succulents

Copyright © 2025 Creative Arts Management OÜ
All rights reserved.

Author: Amelia Montgomery
ISBN HARDBACK: 978-1-80581-713-0
ISBN PAPERBACK: 978-1-80581-240-1
ISBN EBOOK: 978-1-80581-713-0

Life in the Arid

Thirsty plants with spiky hats,
Telling jokes in tiny chats.
Cactus comedies abound,
Laughing at the desert ground.

Sandy floors and sunlit days,
Succulent pranks and silly ways.
When rain clouds show, they leap and dance,
With happy spines, they take a chance.

Sips of Sunlight

Succulents sip their golden brew,
Giggling as the sun shines through.
Tiny teacups in the sand,
Gathering sunshine, oh so grand.

Dancing leaves in shady spots,
Throwing shade at tangled knots.
Oh, to bask in warmth divine,
With silly grins and roots that twine.

Mosaic of Resilience

A patchwork quilt of greens and hues,
Thriving on the sun's good news.
Cracking jokes and growing tall,
Each little plant with spiky gall.

Tales of drought they'll reminisce,
While plotting how to grow in bliss.
Lively bunches, quirky crew,
In the heat, they always renew.

Dreams of Drought

When the skies are clear and bright,
Succulents dream of late-night bites.
To sip the moonlight, sweet and fine,
While plotting snappy little lines.

They laugh at storms that pass them by,
With roots that dance and spirits high.
In this dry land, they find their joy,
A leafy laughter they employ.

The Language of Aloe

Aloe says, "I'm not too thirsty,"
In fact, I sip like it's the worst-y.
I stretch my leaves, a sunlit grin,
In this pot where wild tales begin.

Whispers of soil, a dance with the breeze,
I chat with cacti, they call me 'Queen of Ease.'
With prickly mates who poke and tease,
Together we bloom, oh what a breeze!

Tufts of Time

Time ticks slowly in my succulent crib,
Each leaf a moment, a tiny fib.
I wait for rain, I plead the sun,
This pot life's odd, but oh so fun!

The clock's a joke, it spins like a top,
With every tiny sprout, I just can't stop.
Petals giggle, as they stretch and sway,
In this leafy joke where time's the play!

Harmony in Hues

Green and purple, a quirky crew,
Dancing in pots, what a colorful view!
With orange blooms that simply can't stop,
We throw a party, let's shake the crop!

Laughter in petals, colors collide,
This garden's a canvas, we take great pride.
A little distraction, a vibrant game,
We giggle together, all the same!

Blooming Silence

In stillness, we flourish, by moonlight's grace,
Green thumbs swirl, we all find a place.
Silence bursts with laughter so grand,
In our leafy realm, we take a stand.

Jokes on the wind, whispers take flight,
With each morning sun shining so bright.
Puns in the petals, nature's own art,
In this quiet giggle, we all play our part.

A Canvas of Breath

In pots they sit, an artful bunch,
Green and spiky, each one a punch.
Cacti wear hats, oh what a sight,
Prickly puns bring pure delight!

Aloe drinks tea, with sage and thyme,
Chatting away, they're having a rhyme.
Sedums laugh, they wiggle and dance,
In succulent jams, they take a chance!

Jade plants gossip about the sun,
Sipping on rays, they have their fun.
Potted jokes, they can't stand straight,
With roots so deep, they feel first-rate!

So raise a glass to this quirky crew,
In leafy greens, their spirits brew.
Life's little blooms, they paint the air,
With every chuckle, a love to share!

Fossilized Florals

Dusty relics, a garden's pride,
Succulents fossilized, they won't subside.
Once full of life, now they just sit,
Waiting for jokes, or a good bit!

Lizards lounge on their ancient grace,
Making history, with a smiley face.
Rocky humor in sunlit nooks,
Turning old stones into funny books!

Businesses booming in desert fairies,
Selling dreams with quirky queries.
With every leaf, stories untold,
In hieroglyphs of green and gold!

So tip your hat and tip your drink,
To flora's past, give it a wink.
Eternal giggles in stony beds,
Where laughter thrives and joy spreads!

Portrait of Persistence

In pots of green, they stand so proud,
With spines and leaves, they form a crowd.
Water me? Please! I'll skip that chore,
I'm tougher than you, just check the score.

With every drip, they scoff and jest,
Their secret? 'Survive! It's just the best!'
While others wilt in summer's blaze,
These quirky plants join in the craze.

Serenity in Succulence

A succulent's smile, wide and round,
Basking in sunlight, it's quite renowned.
With leaves like pillows, oh so soft,
One hug could lift you, send you aloft!

They shimmy and shake, a jolly crew,
Exuding calm like morning dew.
"What's your secret?" you might implore,
"Just chill, my friend! We've got galore!"

Cacti's Call

Hey, prickly friend, do you feel the thrill?
With arms raised high, you've got the chill.
Your spines may scare, but I see the grace,
In this desert dance, we've found our place.

The world thinks you're harsh, but they don't know,
You throw the best parties; watch you glow!
With all your charm, you wear a grin,
Better grab a drink, let the fun begin!

Echoes of Earth

In the dance of the dusty terrain,
Echoes of laughter, free from disdain.
"Thirsty?" they ask, with a cheeky wink,
"No thank you," they say, "we prefer to think!"

They whisper of wisdom, so funny and bright,
"Poke us, we dare you, it'll be alright!"
In gardens of joy, they stand with pride,
Witty little wonders, oh what a ride!

The Succulent Waltz

In pots they prance with spiky glee,
Dancing leaves like a jubilee.
They shimmy under the sun's embrace,
In their green attire, they find their place.

With every twist, they shake their stems,
Sipping water like fancy gems.
Their roots tap dance in joyful cheer,
Who knew plants could hold a beer?

Nature's Resilience

In the desert heat, they laugh and thrive,
Surviving with style, they come alive.
Worn-out shoes on a cactus throne,
Living life to the fullest, never alone.

With prickly hugs and hearty grins,
They pull off battles, where no one wins.
Unfazed by drought, they raise their hands,
Nature's jesters in sun-baked lands.

Swaying in Stillness

In perfect rows, they stand so still,
Like they're waiting for a tickle or thrill.
With leaves like fans, they keep the beat,
A silent groove that can't be beat.

The wind teases with a gentle nudge,
But they just giggle, won't even budge.
Balancing sun and a tickle of shade,
In a game of 'who's the most laid'.

Shadows of Agave

In the moonlight's glow, they stretch and sway,
Casting shadows that dance and play.
With serrated edges, they seem to grin,
"Come join the party, let the fun begin!"

Oh, what a sight, the agave parade,
Waving their arms in a playful charade.
They whisper secrets, oh so sly,
"Who knew being thorny could feel so spry?"

Dune Dancers

In the desert, spines stand tall,
Throwing shade, they don't care at all.
A cactus prances, does a little jig,
While the lizards laugh, 'Isn't he big?'

With each sway, they shake and tease,
Tickled by the summer breeze.
Their blooms pop out, a colorful show,
'Can't touch this!' they strut, with a glow.

Oasis of Colors

In a land where sunshine reigns,
Colors burst like runaway trains.
A party of plants, oh what a sight,
They giggle and gloat, feeling just right.

Pink and green in a dance so bright,
'Who wore it best?' they argue with delight.
They sway and wiggle, a lively blend,
In this vibrant land, the fun won't end.

Subtle Strength

Tiny roots hold a towering stance,
Their silent might makes others glance.
With a wink, they whisper, 'We're tough as nails,'
In the face of the wind, each one prevails.

With a jolt of humor, they rise with pride,
Cracking jokes like a plant-based guide.
'You think you can break us? Just give it a go!'
They chuckle and sway, putting on a show.

Silent Blooms

In twilight's hush, they make their scene,
Softly giggling, so sly and serene.
Petals unfurl, like a wink in the night,
'Bet you didn't see us until the light!'

With a bashful blush, they peek and sway,
If candlelit dinners aren't here to stay.
Owning the night, they subtly tease,
'Find us, dear friends, if you please!'

Thorns and Tranquility

When you poke me with your prickle,
I giggle like a silly tickle.
Those spikes can't dampen my delight,
I'm thriving here, feeling just right.

In pots we sit, a quirky crew,
Each with our story, all brand new.
I dance in sun with my green friends,
Who needs a garden? This pot transcends!

Watch out for the one named Spikey,
He's known for being a bit too hikey.
But don't you worry, it's all in jest,
In this plant banter, we all are blessed.

So come join us, bring some cheer,
With laughter, joy, and maybe beer.
In our green world, we all blend,
Thorns and tranquility, never end.

Echoes in Green

In the desert where we thrive,
Listen close, hear us jive!
We rustle leaves, chat in the breeze,
A succulent band, we do as we please.

Cactuses whisper their secrets low,
About the sun and the rain's sweet flow.
Puns about roots and stems take flight,
Each spiky laugh, a pure delight.

Under moonlight, we hold a show,
Dancing shadows, in a row.
Don't trip on the thorns, they're just for fun,
Join the green giggle till the night is done.

So if you're sad, come take a peek,
Into our world where we often speak.
In echoes bright, we find our glee,
A garden of laughter, wild and free.

Lullabies of Lifeblood

In the quiet hours when light fades,
We sing of life in leafy parades.
Our lullabies sway in the gentle night,
Under stars, everything feels right.

Sprouts of laughter from little pots,
Tickling roots in adventurous knots.
Sleep, dear friend, in your cozy bed,
Dream of succulents dancing in your head.

Whispers of water, a caring tune,
As we sip sunlight, beneath the moon.
A nightly pact, to grow and to play,
In this botanical fun, we'll sway all day.

So rest your eyes, let worries slow,
In this symphony of green, let love flow.
With each little leaf, we'll sing you soft lies,
In lullabies of lifeblood, where joy never dies.

Cacti Serenade

In a pot where the sunlight streams,
Growin' tall like we're livin' dreams.
With spiky hats, we sing our song,
In this prickly place, we all belong.

Tap tap tap, on the window pane,
Hear our harmony like a funny train.
We jump and jiggle, roots all a-twist,
Dance like no one's watching, we can't resist!

The desert's our stage, we shine and glow,
With little thorns that steal the show.
Cacti friends, let's strike a pose,
Swaying wildly, in colorful clothes.

So gather 'round, we're here to play,
Our spiny fun will brighten your day.
In the land of green, where quirkiness resides,
Dancing cacti are the best of guides!

Resilient Beauty

In a pot on the sill, they grin so wide,
Each leaf like a smile, none can hide.
They drink with a sip, a gentle sip,
Sunbathing in glory, they never flip.

Cactus in the corner, wearing a hat,
Says, 'I'm so spiky, aren't I a brat?'
With friends like these, what's the fuss?
We grow in the chaos, it's all a plus!

Petals of Persistence

Little green warriors fight through the heat,
Plantling gossip fills every street.
'Did you see that bloom? It's quite a hoot!'
Petals of green, ain't life just cute?

Let's throw a party, with soil and light,
Dance on the windowsill, through day and night.
Though sometimes we flop, we'll just redecorate,
Because we're resilient, and life's just great!

Melodic Thicket

In the garden, a thicket so bright,
Each succulent singing, oh what a sight!
'Be aware of my thorns!' they all shout,
While tossing their leaves about all about!

A little jade giggles, 'I'm part of a band!'
With aloe and agave, they take a stand.
Their tunes filled with laughter, like children at play,
In this quirky garden, no dull day!

The Art of Succor

In the art of support, we've mastered the game,
Sharing our sunshine, never the same.
When one feels a drought, we just lend some rain,
With giggles and grins, we'll lighten the strain.

We trade leaves for laughter, that's how we thrive,
Wiggling our roots, we're truly alive.
In pots of delight, let's make it a spree,
For in this wild world, we're family!

The Quiet Bloom

In a pot of dreams, they sit quite still,
With the grace of dancers, they bend at will.
One's wearing a hat, the other a shoe,
I think they're planning a garden debut.

Their roots intertwine, a tangled affair,
Whispering secrets like they just don't care.
The sun peeks in, a judge with a grin,
While they play hide-and-seek, let the games begin.

In the corner of chaos, they find some peace,
Each succulent giggles, their laughter won't cease.
With sassy little smiles, they take center stage,
In the world of the weird, they turn a new page.

As the water drops dance, oh what a sight,
They sip their punch under moon's soft light.
These little green jesters, a playful crew,
In their leafy kingdom, they welcome you too.

Prickled Poetry

In a world full of thorns, they wear their spikes,
With a flick of a leaf, they tell all the hikes.
One's throwing shade, the other's a tease,
Prickled poetry flows like a warm summer breeze.

Cacti confess their love for the sun,
While succulents sing, "Let's have some fun!"
With each little quirk, they're quite the charmer,
Making gardens giggle, their wit just a armor.

Under the radar, they plot and scheme,
Living out loud in a botanical dream.
With stems all a-wobble, and colors so bright,
They dance in their pots, a heartwarming sight.

In the green gallery, they paint the air,
With playful intent, they spread joyful flair.
These prickly personas, they know how to bloom,
Creating a laughter, that brightens the room.

Oasis of Serenity

In a silent desert, they find their peace,
Chillin' with style, their joy won't cease.
Sipping sunshine and soaking the rays,
In this still haven, they spend their days.

Each leaf a joke, each stem a pun,
In the land of easy, they're having fun.
They whisper "hush" as the breezes blow,
Spreading calm vibes like a sweet undertow.

With colors so vivid, a palette of cheer,
They twirl in the wind without any fear.
Creating an oasis that's cozy and bright,
These green little buddies bring pure delight.

So when life's a storm, and chaos is near,
Just glance at their charm, and know they are here.
In this placid garden where laughter is free,
Enjoy the serenity, come plant with me.

Threads of Green

In the fabric of life, they weave with flair,
Nature's own stitchers, with prickles to spare.
Twisting and turning, they spin a good yarn,
Crafting a legend beneath the big barn.

Their colors collide in a humorous dance,
In this patch of giggles, they take every chance.
From desert to kitchen, they make quite the scene,
Adorning our spaces with threads of green.

Hilarity blooms in each little spout,
With a twist of their trunk, they banish all doubt.
These playful plants have a story to tell,
In their leafy realm, all is merry and well.

So join in the fun, grab a pot and a spoon,
Let's stir up some laughter beneath the bright moon.
For in this green patch, life's so keen,
It's a tapestry woven with threads of green.

Nature's Palette in Harmony

In pots they dance with glee,
Each prickly friend so bold.
With colors bright and free,
They're stories to be told.

Cacti wear a funny hat,
A sombrero made of clay.
Succulents share a hearty chat,
About the sun's buffet.

Aloes wave like fans of cheer,
As laughter fills the air.
The world is full of cheer,
When you've got plants to share!

In this quirky garden scene,
Jade leaves chuckle on the side.
With every silly green routine,
Life's a fun-filled ride.

The Arid Chord Progression.

In the land where dry winds blow,
    Jumpy cacti start to sway.
They've got a dance move flow,
    That brightens up the day.

With sleek and shiny skins,
    They're nature's standup show.
Spikey jokes, where laughter spins,
    Under the sun's warm glow.

Graptopetalum's sneaky grin,
    Cracks up the pinky crew.
While Echeveria dives right in,
    To steal the spotlight too.

Join the concert of the sprout,
    With melodies of green.
Who knew a desert drought
    Could create such a scene?

Whispers of Jade

Whispers travel through the air,
Jade leaves gossip on display.
In this garden, joy's the flair,
With every branching sway.

They giggle when the breezes blow,
And chuckle at the rain.
"Hey, don't let the water flow,
We're excellent at pain!"

Little succulents conspire,
Hatching plots in green delight.
"Let's set this dull day afire,
With humor shining bright!"

So, under the sun's sweet care,
They dance and sing with style.
Joy blooms in the open air,
Let's laugh a little while.

Desert Melodies

In a garden filled with cheer,
Succulents sing their tune.
With ribs so sharp, and green so sheer,
They blend beneath the moon.

Outlaws of the sandy land,
Rogues with spines of fun.
Just when you think they've planned,
They're dancing one by one.

Chubby leaves all sway in line,
Each a jester in disguise.
With roots that twist and strain,
They flirt without a sigh.

In this sun-drenched harmony,
Where arid laughter reigns.
Even rocks join in, you see,
When humor breaks the chains.

When Leaves Speak Softly

In the pot, a cactus grins,
Wearing spines like tiny pins.
It whispers tales of sunny days,
Of cheeky ants and sunlit rays.

A jade plant sways with glee,
Sharing jokes with a hearty tree.
They laugh till the shadows grow long,
In their quirky, green-filled throng.

Succulents chat with a giggle and tease,
While sipping dew from the warm spring breeze.
They rally for a sunbathing spot,
Unfazed by the heat, they're quite the lot.

When rain drops fall, they do a dance,
Doing the twist in joyful prance.
Who knew greens could be so spry?
In this garden, laugh we must try!

Chorus of the Succulent Quartet

Four little pots on a sunny shelf,
Singing tunes of a jovial self.
A spiky friend croons a high-pitch note,
While a soft leaf dips, doing the boat.

The haworthia hums a mellow song,
Echoing where the silly belong.
With every sway, a leaf outstretched,
Their raucous laughter, perfectly etched.

The sedum joins with a grateful smile,
Their harmony spreads for quite a mile.
They tease the air with tunes so bright,
Under the twinkling stars at night.

In their cute little voices, they sway,
Making sure to brighten the day.
A quartet that grows in sunshine cheer,
With friends like these, there's nothing to fear!

Interlude in the Garden

In the midst of vibrant greens,
A leafy ensemble plots and schemes.
With idle leaves, they giggle and chat,
Swapping stories of weather and brat.

The succulent here can surely prattle,
Casting shadows, no room for glad rattle.
A palm leaf recounts tales of the breeze,
While the aloe spills secrets with ease.

Each corner sings with pointed wit,
These brutes of the garden sure throw a fit.
Jokes about water, oh aren't they sly!
In a drought, these guys still dare to fly!

The interlude flows with a chuckle here,
Bringing smiles, watering each fear.
For in this plot of green and cheer,
Life is a stage, the fun is near!

The Harmony of Drought Resistance

Here's a tale of the desert crew,
Living large, in the sun, they grew.
Water's scarce, but they don't fuss,
In their tiny hearts, there's always a plus.

A barrel cactus, plump and round,
Sings low, while the others bound.
"I'll be fine, I'm full of flair,
And I've got spines to spare!"

The echeveria looks quite chic,
Feathers of pink, it's no mystique.
In the shade it giggles, just having fun,
Turning heads while basking in sun.

Drought may come, and drought may go,
This garden's pride will brilliantly glow.
They toast to life, with roots held tight,
In a world of green, all is just right!

Secrets of the Succulent

In a pot under the sun, they dwell,
Whispers of leaves, secrets to tell.
Cacti wearing hats, quite a sight,
With spines like jokes that prick with delight.

Chasing the sun, they stretch and sway,
Belly laugh as shadows play.
Sipping water, just a drop, you see,
These green warriors thrive so carefreely.

Plant parents giggle, feeling so proud,
Root systems chatting, cozy and loud.
When it rains, they have a dance,
In puddles of joy, they take a chance.

With colors bright, they dress in style,
Each little sprout brings a smile.
Secrets so sweet, they share with glee,
Succulent shenanigans, wild and free.

Rise of the Resilient

Up from the soil, they boldly rise,
With tiny arms stretched to the skies.
Each little leaf, a warrior's shield,
Ready to conquer, never to yield.

Riding the wind, they wiggle and jive,
In every challenge, they learn to thrive.
With a chuckle, they face the drought,
A little green humor's what it's about.

When pests come knocking, what a surprise,
These spunky plants don't compromise.
With a wiggle and jiggle, they shoo away
Those pesky bugs that want to play.

So here's to the resilient, full of flair,
In sunshine and storm, they're always there.
With roots in the ground and laughs in the air,
They teach us to bloom, even in despair.

Verdant Visions

Picture this, in a patch of green,
Succulents smiling, what a scene!
A gathering of friends, we must agree,
Planted gossip, oh so comically.

Every shape, a quirky face,
Some with style, others in grace.
They giggle softly under the sun,
A gathering here is all in good fun.

As shadows waltz across the ground,
They tell tall tales without a sound.
With roots intertwined, a secret pact,
In the world of plants, laughter's an act.

Blushing blooms and thorny jokes,
In their own world, a bunch of folks.
With verdant visions, they light the dark,
Leaves filled with humor, each leaf a spark.

The Gentle Vigor

In the sunny spots where they bask,
These gentle giants, no easy task.
Seedlings sprouting, a sight to behold,
With humor tucked in, not all that bold.

Total chill, they grow with ease,
Shaking off worries like autumn leaves.
Each stretch and curl, a comedy show,
With laughter, they green up the row.

When thirsty dreams come creeping by,
They take a sip and wink an eye.
Belly laughs in sandy beds,
They know the joy of leafy spreads.

With gentle vigor, they stand so tall,
In a world of chaos, they call to all.
Softly giggling in the light, so bright,
These playful plants bring pure delight.

Melodic Reflections in Sunlight

In the garden they gleam, oh what a show,
Cacti in hats, putting on quite the glow.
They sip on their sunshine, quite the fine feast,
With the breeze as their buddy, they twirl, they feast.

Wobbly and round, they bounce in delight,
Chasing the shadows, they dance in the light.
Glorious giggles erupt from the blooms,
As they plot out their mischief amidst their perfumes.

Tiny green soldiers, standing so proud,
Pop out their heads, they're never too cowed.
Tickled by petals, they sway to the beat,
In this whimsical world, they just can't be beat.

So luscious, so quirky, these sap-filled chums,
Creating sweet chaos, they sway like drum thumps.
Amidst prickly laughter, they share a good cheer,
This garden of mirth, where all friends draw near.

A Dance of Drought Survivors

Gather round, oh the dry and the proud,
With their spiky attire, they'll charm any crowd.
In a jig of survival, they shimmy and shake,
Through the heat of the sun, their coolness they make.

Performing their tricks in brightly lit shows,
Who knew that a cactus could bust out some flows?
With their succulent moves and rhythm divine,
They spin through the heat like good friends of mine.

Teetering gently, so hearty and bold,
The agave whispers, "Come join, be consoled!"
They swap silly stories, share water in dreams,
In a sassy drought dance, they plot in their schemes.

Adventurous spirits, they thrive on the cheer,
With a twist and a turn, they swallow their fear.
In the land of the thriving, they're kings of the scene,
These drought-slaying dancers, so happy and keen.

Visual Verses from the Desert

In a canvas of green, the art takes its form,
Where spines tell a tale, through the heat, they perform.
Each moment a brushstroke, so colorful, bright,
An exhibition of life in the shimmering light.

Petals that giggle, and leaves full of gleam,
Playful companions, it seems like a dream.
With a swirling of sand, they dance with the breeze,
Painting pictures of joy, amongst prickly tease.

The lizards join in, clapping claws in delight,
While the sun casts its glow, all is merry and bright.
With mischievous smiles, they conspire and cheer,
These odd little dwellers have nothing to fear.

From the soil they emerge, with gusto, they play,
They live for the laughter, come join in their fray!
In quirky formations, they shimmer and sway,
In this vivid fiesta, they're leading the way.

Symphony of Resilience

Prickled companions in a sunbeam parade,
With charm and tenacity, never afraid.
They wave tiny flags, with water as gold,
In a drought-touched land, their stories unfold.

Daring and feisty, they laugh at the heat,
Who knew being spiky could look so neat?
They outlast the dry spells, they take it in stride,
While sharing their secrets, with laughter as guide.

Elixirs of green, with sunsets they toast,
Rooted in soil, they're truly engrossed.
Through giggles and sun, they sprout an attire,
In this wacky world, they sparkle with fire.

They'll dry up the tears, turn them into cheer,
With each mighty bloom, their stories we share.
The desert's bright symphony, it sings from within,
In laughter and joy, let the fun now begin!

Textured Tunes of the Earth

In a pot, the cacti dance,
Twirling spines in a goofy prance.
A succulent's giggle, oh so spry,
Makes every gardener laugh and sigh.

A jade plant strums on a leaf-guitar,
While the aloe sings from near and far.
The soil's beat is funky and wild,
As every plant behaves like a child.

Underneath the desert sun,
Their funny faces make gardening fun.
With leaves like hats, they tip and bow,
Who knew plants could take a bow?

So here's to whimsies that grow and thrive,
In every pot, their joy comes alive.
With prickly charm and colors bright,
They spread their whimsical delight!

Nature's Quiet Orchestra

The succulents gather, but wait, oh no!
The maestro is a snail moving slow.
With a rhythmic shrug, they sway to the beat,
As the wind whispers secrets, oh so sweet.

A plump little rosette, full of flair,
Winks at a cactus with dance moves rare.
The yucca chimes in with a clunky twirl,
While the agave does a slow-motion swirl.

Laughter erupts from every green face,
As they prance about in their little space.
A harmony of leaves, strangely neat,
Making music that's oh so upbeat.

Each leaf a note in this garden song,
All are welcome, come dance along.
With nature's rhythm, we giggle and sway,
In this quirky concert, we'll play all day!

The Unfolding Leaves

A tender bud bursts with glee,
Like a magician shouting, "Look at me!"
Each leaf unravels, spreads with cheer,
Whispering secrets for all to hear.

A prickly party, full of delight,
Cactus wearing a crown, what a sight!
With every twist and every turn,
A fun-filled tale, eager to learn.

The leaves unfold like a joke with a pun,
"Who's the funniest plant? Just wait for the sun!"
A festival of textures, oh so sly,
Just watch 'em laugh as the days drift by.

In the garden stage, they steal the show,
With sap and smiles, they put on a glow.
So here's to leaves that unravel and grin,
What funny wonders these plants tuck in!

Sonnet of the Spines

Within the pots, they stick and poke,
A spiny laughter that's no joke.
With sharp remarks and silly jabs,
They tease each other with playful grabs.

A spiney debate, who's pointier still?
The agave boasts with a cheeky thrill.
While the barrel plant rolls with glee,
"I'm round and proud, come laugh with me!"

With tender hearts wrapped in comedy,
Each prickly friend shares a fun story.
Their zany quirks and quirky charms,
Bring giggles crackling like garden alarms.

So let's applaud these verdant hearts,
With antics playful, they win our smarts.
In a world of green, let the laughter climb—
For spines can be funny, one poke at a time!

Echoing Succulents

In pots they sit, a merry crew,
With eyes of jade and shades of blue.
They whisper jokes, they poke and tease,
As sunlight spills, they giggle with ease.

Some grow tall, while others are stout,
A never-ending, leafy bout.
In cactus arms, a hug they give,
These plucky plants know how to live.

With every sip of morning dew,
They share their tales, both old and new.
"Why did the cactus cross the road?"
"To show off spikes, it's quite a load!"

So let them thrive, in light and bloom,
These funny greens will chase the gloom.
With laughter sprouting from each leaf,
They spark joy, what a green belief!

Enchanted Prickles

Once I met a spiky sage,
Who wore a hat — oh what a page!
Each needle told a funny story,
Of sun and rain, in all its glory.

A party planned in garden beds,
Where prickly friends would nod their heads.
"Bring the water, we'll have a blast!
Just watch your feet, they're spiked, so fast!"

Cat grasses dance, with laughter loud,
While senecios wear a proud shroud.
"Let's salsa now," the agave cried,
And all the greens just swirled and sighed.

So if you think they're dull or meek,
These prickles here are far from weak.
In every pot, there's fun to find,
With sharp-witted greens that blow your mind!

Textures of Time

Oh, the wrinkles on my leafy friends,
Tell stories of seasons that never ends.
They stretch and squish, like dough in hand,
In their wise age, hard to withstand.

Succulents wear the passage grand,
With quirks and dips across the land.
"Who needs a doctor? I've got my sun!
With each slow sip, my day is fun!"

Each layer thick with laughter wrapped,
They chuckle softly, never trapped.
With colors bright, they paint the day,
In textures rich, they laugh and play.

Embrace their forms, so dense and fine,
In every twist, a hidden line.
Together we'll grow, in humor and rhyme,
These silly greens, they bide their time!

The Warmth of Green

In sunny spots, my plants do bask,
With winks and nods is all I ask.
Their leaves so plump, like jellybeans,
They crack me up with funny scenes.

When potted pals regale a tale,
Of scaling heights and storms that pale.
"Who needs rain when we have cheer?
With cactus cups, let's drink a beer!"

The jade and clay, a joyous mix,
With laughter shared in every fix.
"Who's got the dirt? Let's start a fight!
The winner slays with roots so tight!"

So here's to hues of vibrant grace,
In every nook, they find their place.
With warmth so rich, they crack a smile,
In every leaf, they go the extra mile!

Rhythms of the Drought

In pots they sit, all lined in a row,
Cacti in hats, putting on quite a show.
They chirp and they chuckle, a quirky delight,
While sipping on sunbeams from morning to night.

With shallow roots, they wiggle and sway,
"Water? Nah, not today!" they giggle and play.
A drought is a party, a chance to unwind,
They toast with their thorns, 'To dry days, we're blind!'

Vibrant Verses in Green

All green and pointy, with laughter they tease,
"Don't let my spikes fool you, I'm soft as a breeze!"
Playing hide and seek, under wide desert skies,
With playful blooms popping, oh what a surprise!

One's strutting around, like a cactus on stage,
Twirling its arms, just to act its own age.
"Stay hydrated!" it shouts, "My fruit's quite the treat,
But beware of my prickles—be it bitter or sweet!"

The Refrain of Resilience

Sipping the sunshine, swaying with glee,
These charming green pals laugh, 'Come dance with me!'
With roots in the ground, they're never in doubt,
"Survival is easy, just let it all out!"

Their laughter is stirring, like wind through the leaves,
"Don't mind the weeds, they're just wearing bad sleeves!"

With every dry chuckle, the world makes a sound,
"For moisture in laughter, we've turned it around!"

Tones of Tranquility

With colors so vibrant, they hold quite a tune,
"Join in with our chorus, you sun-baked buffoon!"
Giggles emerge from spiky green stones,
As they bask in the glow, they revel in tones.

A choir of succulents, full of charm and cheer,
Playing musical chairs, without any fear.
"Forget all your worries, let's dance in the heat,
For we are the party—no need to compete!"

Quiet Resonance

In a pot, they sit so still,
Little greens with laughter to spill.
Cacti chuckle, their spines all prickle,
Jade and aloe share a tickle.

Succulent shenanigans all around,
In a garden with joy unbound.
They whisper secrets, oh-so-keen,
In their world, they've made a scene.

Pineapple sage is dancing tall,
While turtle vines follow her call.
Each leaf has a story, a quirky jest,
In their green realm, they never rest.

So listen close to the planty choir,
Their jokes and puns never tire.
With pots of giggles, let's unite,
In this verdant world, pure delight.

Vibrant Solitude

Alone they sit, they rule the shelf,
Each one a treasure, a living elf.
With shades of green, they play and sway,
Making solitude a funny play.

A single leaf starts to complain,
"Why must I grow in such a lane?"
The tiny sprout next to him grins,
"At least we don't have to wear pins!"

The rubber plant's got a meme or two,
With a smile that's bright, and that's quite true.
They hold debates on watering woes,
And giggle at the way each sprouts and grows.

So here's to those who grow alone,
In their pot, they've found a throne.
With every twist and every bend,
They've made this green world their best friend.

Starlit Terrariums

In glassy homes, they twinkle bright,
Cacti giggle in the starlit night.
Ferns make jokes about the moon,
In their crystal world, they sing a tune.

A pet rock joins for a stellar show,
Spouting puns, with no reason to slow.
"Why did the plant bring a lamp?" he jokes,
"To light up the room with its leafy folks!"

Tiny stars in the jars all hum,
While squishy succulents dance to the drum.
Mossy maracas shake with delight,
In this glass haven, they party all night.

They've formed a band, quite unreal,
With each little leaf adding to the feel.
In starlit terrariums, fun's the game,
Where every plant brings its own claim to fame.

Green Wisdom

In the heart of green, knowledge grows,
Succulents wise with their leafy prose.
"Water me less, and I shall thrive,"
They share their secrets, sweet and alive.

Aloe's wisdom, soft and bright,
Says laughter grows in morning light.
"Prickly pears know how to chill,
Just sit in the sun and enjoy the thrill!"

The jade plant teaches financial grace,
"Save your energy, don't race!
In stillness, wealth will find its way,
Green dreams bloom, come what may!"

So gather 'round, take heed, my friends,
Listen to the green, as laughter bends.
In every word, a joke is spun,
With leafy wisdom, life is fun!

Textured Tales

In pots so bright, they stand so proud,
With spiky hats, they draw a crowd.
Each green twist tells a silly joke,
While sunlight makes them laugh and poke.

Their cousin cactus wears a grin,
Rubbing elbows with chubby kin.
A dance of thorns and plump delight,
These flora jesters steal the light.

Oh, how they wiggle in the breeze,
With tiny arms that sway with ease.
They whisper secrets, soft and sly,
About the butterflies floating by.

So let us cheer for these funny plants,
With quirky shapes and silly chants.
In the garden, they reign supreme,
A textured tale, a dreamer's dream.

Prickle and Peace

Oh prickly friend, you're quite the sight,
In gardens glowing with morning light.
You promise peace with just one glance,
But touch too close, you start to prance.

The gentle jades sway to and fro,
While thorns play tag with seeds that grow.
In this zany dance, they spin around,
A prickly peace and joy unbound.

With laughter spilling from their leaves,
They tickle hearts and play with thieves.
Keep your hands in pockets, stay alert,
These happy shrubs can really hurt!

So here's to plants with attitude bold,
Whose funny quirks are worth more than gold.
In every prick lies a secret smile,
Embrace the chaos, stay awhile!

Vitality in Stillness

While others rush in frantic dance,
These green folks flaunt their quiet stance.
In silence, they tap into pure glee,
Exuding charm as calm as can be.

One winks with fluff, another with spikes,
Each one beams, "Take life's little hikes!"
A merry heart in stillness found,
With roots so deep, they laugh around.

They whisper tales of slow, sweet days,
As sun-soaked afternoons turn to rays.
Vitality dances in every hue,
With every pause, they bloom anew.

In this calm kingdom, time stands still,
Who needs a rush when you've got will?
A vibrant show of laughter and light,
In stillness, these plants shine so bright!

The Sober Green

In a world so wild, they wear their hue,
A sober crew, with comical view.
Standing tall, they puff out their chests,
Making sure they get all the best quests.

"Why so serious?" a leaf confides,
While others giggle and roll their sides.
"No need to fret, we've weathered all,
In our green realm, we never fall."

With a twist and curl, they tell a tale,
Of storms and droughts and funny fails.
Their steady vibe, a laugh in disguise,
Amidst the chaos, they're truly wise.

Cheers to the plants who stay composed,
With giggles tucked beneath their prose.
The sober green, a jolly sight,
In every pot, a laugh ignites!

Compositions in Clay Pots

In pots where greens gather round,
Cacti laugh without a sound.
Succulents share their quirky tales,
As they wiggle in sunny gales.

A jade plant dances to the beat,
While aloe sways, feeling the heat.
Their spiky hugs bring so much cheer,
Plant party vibes, all through the year.

In sunlight, their colors pop bright,
Each leaf having its own little light.
With each gurgle from the root,
They gossip like a flowered hoot.

Yet be careful, oh dear friend,
For prickles can be round the bend.
These silly greens will make you chuckle,
With all their hues and sprightly shuffle.

Echoes of Flora's Resurgence

Booming blooms in pots that stand,
Whisper secrets, oh so grand.
Each succulent, a playful elf,
Pretending to be wise itself.

A plump one says, 'I'm quite the star!
Just look at my leaves! Look at me spar!'
While skinny ones just roll their eyes,
Claiming they're the calmest guys.

In their world of playful vibes,
They joke of water, sun, and jibes.
Oregonia drops a joke or two,
While spiky friends just laugh for the view.

As they bask in light of day,
These amusing greens, they splay and sway.
In pot-bound glee, let laughter glee,
For nature's quirks are always free!

Soft Beats of Nature's Palette

A rhythmic rustle, soft and sweet,
Timid leaves dance to the beat.
Succulents sway in amber light,
Spinning tales all through the night.

Plump globes giggle, 'Look at us!
We're the quirkiest, no need to fuss.'
As spiky flags begin to sway,
They start a fun, wild cabaret.

In hues of green and hints of red,
They spin around, pounding their head.
These leafy jokers, oh what a sight,
A nightly riot of pure delight.

So pot them up and let them shine,
A chorus of fun, oh so divine.
With tiny voices, they share the news,
That nature's colors will always amuse!

Cascades of Verdant Spirits

From shady nooks to sunbeam spots,
These greens bring joy to weary thoughts.
Each leaf is like a tiny cheer,
Whispering fun, oh come near!

Eagerly lined in a joyful row,
Spiky pals in a colorful show.
Each one striking a pose so bold,
With stories of warmth that never get old.

In terracotta, they wiggle and shake,
'Water me not, for laughter's at stake!'
They prank the gardener with gentle grins,
While basking in light as mischief begins.

So if you're feeling a bit down low,
Join in their fun; let the giggles flow.
For in this green, lively parade,
Are whispers of joy that will never fade.

www.ingramcontent.com/pod-product-compliance
Lightning Source LLC
Chambersburg PA
CBHW072135070526
44585CB00016B/1685